HEALING OUR LOSSES

A JOURNAL FOR WORKING THROUGH YOUR GRIEF

Jack Miller, PhD

Resource Publications, Inc.
San Jose, California

Editorial director: Kenneth Guentert
Managing editor: Elizabeth J. Asborno
Editorial assistant: Lisa Hernandez
Cover design and illustrations: Sr. Terri Davis
Back cover photograph: Mary Donlan
Cover production: Huey Lee

Reprint Department
Resource Publications, Inc.
160 E. Virginia Street #290
San Jose, CA 95112-5876

Library of Congress Cataloging in Publication Data
Miller, Jack, 1945-
   Healing our losses : a journal for working through your grief / Jack
Miller.
       p.   cm.
   ISBN 0-89390-255-1
   1. Grief—Case studies.   2. Loss (Psychology)—Case studies.
3. Bereavement—Psychological aspects—Case studies.   4. Miller, Jack,
1945- . I. Title.
BF575.G7M53   1993
155.9'37—dc20   92-41564

97 96 95 94 93 | 5 4 3 2 1

To all of those who have parented me
(physically, emotionally, and spiritually).
May my life's work be a tribute to their generosity.

CONTENTS

To the Caregiver

If you are helping others through the grieving process and plan to use this book with an invidivual or in a group setting, let me begin by thanking you for choosing *Healing Our Losses* as your text. I would highly encourage you to work through the entire eight-step process yourself (adhering to the instructions set out in the introductory letter that follows) before attempting to lead others along this path. I trust that you know that you cannot take anyone where you have not gone yourself. That is particularly true in facilitating grief. Allow these stories to touch you first and then create your own tribute before proceeding any further.

If you find yourself dealing with lots of unresolved grief and at the same time are being requested to help others, consider taking a twelve-week sabbatical and accompanying me through The Phoenix Project. Living arrangements and so on can all be made here in Chicago without any difficulty whatsoever. Participation in The Phoenix Project will enable you to *completely* heal your grief and give you the necessary tools to help others at the same time.

If you feel capable of guiding others through this eight-step process, let me emphasize the value of incorporating regular exercise, meditation, dream interpretation, and creative expression in a ritualized format with your people. All of these are integral aspects of The Phoenix Project, and it does enable people to heal themselves. If you want more information on The Phoenix Project, feel free to write me in care of the publisher:

Dr. Jack Miller
c/o Resource Publications, Inc.
160 E. Virginia Street #290
San Jose, CA 95112-5876

To the Reader

We are about to embark on a journey together that will take us back over the losses of our lives. I have been this way before with many others and I know just how difficult it can be. There will be times when you will not want to go any further, or you may want to skip over a chapter or two. I want to encourage you not to wander off on your own. Take your lead from me, and keep in mind that there really are not any shortcuts to healing unresolved grief. You will discover over time that the tears and the depression are actually important parts of your healing process.

You say that you want to get on with your life. You want to feel like your old self again, with energy to spare. Well, that can happen. We can get there together—just wait and see. In order to move on with your life, we are going to have to go back and stir up all those painful old memories once again. There is no other way!

Our journey together will consist of us sharing the stories of our losses with one another. I will tell you a story from my history, and then you will be asked to share your corresponding story with me. At the end of each story, I will ask you to write about a particular aspect of your own history. My stories and my questions are meant to stir your memories. It will be very important for you to allow yourself to write on and on in response to each question. Write as much as you can possibly remember—no detail is too insignificant to be jotted down. Even though you have been allotted a certain number of pages for writing, do not allow yourself to be limited by the confines of this journal. If you need more space, use your own paper and write as much as you can. Know that the more you write in response to each story, the more you will facilitate your own natural healing process.

There is no way to rush healing. You need to take your own good time. Once you have written absolutely everything you can remember, then set your journal aside for at least three full days before proceeding to the next story. Moving any quicker would only waste your time.

You are asked to wait for at least three days in between each story in order to allow yourself to feel the depression which might well surface along the way. It is essential to let yourself feel the feelings of depression and cry whenever you feel like it. Both the tears and the feelings of depression are facets of your own healing process. Do not try to push them away by distracting yourself with other thoughts or activities. Feeling the pain is what this journey is all about. You need to give yourself permission to cry and to feel depressed. That is part of healing.

The final chapter is not so much about story-telling as it is about making a tribute to your lost loved one. Writing all of these stories will help to prepare you for the tribute-making exercise. Whenever you are ready to proceed, we can begin our journey together.

1

MOTHER

I was born on August 26, 1945, at Father Baker's Orphanage in Lackawanna, New York. The young, unmarried woman who birthed me named me—Eugene William Schultz—and gave me up for adoption. That is all that I know about my origin.

I remained at the orphanage for five months. My crib was one of many, and it stood in the corner of the nursery. I must have always laid in the same position with my back to the wall—looking out toward the motion and the light. When I was adopted, one side of my head was quite flat. I am told that it did not take long for the physical scar to heal; however, it took years to heal the emotional one! I was adopted by Joseph and Edna Miller of Lima, Ohio; they renamed me John Anthony Miller.

From then on in, Edna Miller was my mother; we developed a very strong bond with one another. Mom had not had a particularly easy life. Her parents had only been married for four months, when their car was struck by a train. My grandfather was killed instantly. My grandmother, who was three months pregnant with Mom, was thrown higher than a boxcar and landed on a track—breaking her leg with the fall. She remained in a coma for two weeks; when she regained consciousness, she discovered she was a widow. Due to the pregnancy, her broken leg would not heal properly. She was hospitalized for six months—laying on her back in traction. After she gave birth to my mother, her leg finally healed; however, she walked with a limp the rest of her life. The local newspaper reported that my mother, Edna Marie Steinke, was a "perfectly normal baby."

My grandmother worked as a practical nurse, and mother often had to be left with relatives for long periods of time. Mom was often shifted from one home to another; at one point, she went to four different schools in one year. As a result, my mother was often separated from her mother. This was very painful for both of them, but there was no other way.

A year after my mom and dad were married, my grandmother came down with leukemia. She moved in with my parents so that Mom could take care of her. Grandmother died a very agonizing death, which left my mother emotionally debilitated for quite some time. I was adopted into this household two years later. Is it any wonder that I am inclined to befriend the sick and the dying?

Now, what I want you to do is to write all about your mother. Do not worry about spelling or punctuation. This is your journal. No one else need ever see what is written here. It is important for you to write as much as you possibly can about your mother. You need to reconnect with all of those memories now.

2
FATHER

Whereas my mother was an only child, my father was one of ten children. As a little boy, Joe somehow managed to wander away from a family picnic and got lost in the woods during a sudden downpour. After that, he developed bronchial trouble, which plagued him the rest of his life. As a teenager, his bronchitis was misdiagnosed for tuberculosis; he spent time in a sanatorium, which set him back a year in school.

After high school, Dad took off and hitchhiked out west. This gives you a feel for his independent and adventuresome spirit. When he returned to Ohio, the country was in the midst of the Depression; he took whatever odd jobs he could find in order to survive. He eventually followed in his father's footsteps and hired out as a fireman on the B & O Railroad. A few years later, Dad was promoted to become a railroad engineer. He held that job the rest of his work-life.

Joseph and Edna had been married for five years and could have no children of their own. They applied to Fr. Baker's Orphanage and eventually adopted three children: Jack, Gerry, and Mary. I was their first child, and they certainly had their hands full with me. One of the first things I did was to rock my crib with such force that plaster literally fell from the ceiling. They had to put my mattress onto the floor in order to keep me from destroying the house.

As soon as I was able to crawl, I would crawl across the living room rug and get into the magazine rack. Being very curious, I would take out all of the magazines and make quite a mess. Well, my dad was determined that this little character was not going to disrupt their lives; therefore, he would tell me, "No!" I knew that whenever I would get into the magazine rack, I would be spanked; and yet, I was quite determined to have my own way. I am told that I would cry as I would crawl toward the magazine rack—knowing that I was going to be punished. I am also told that I did not let the fear of punishment stop me!

As I grew older, I got to be rather heavy and did not like competitive sports. This bothered my dad. He was afraid I would be labeled a "sissy." In order to deal with this situation, he set a goal for me to master. I was to chin myself on the clothesline post in our backyard. Well, either I could not or would not do it. Whatever, I was not to leave the backyard, except to go to school, until I chinned myself. Both my father, and myself, were very stubborn. I spent an entire year in my backyard! That should give you a feel for the tug of war between the two of us. I eventually chinned myself in order to escape.

Now, what I want you to do is to write all about your father. Try writing as much as you can possibly remember. It is important to reconnect with all of those memories now.

3

FIRST DEATH

When I was a young boy, my very favorite person in the whole wide world was my grandfather, Benny Miller. He lived down the street on the next block. My grandfather had a deep devotion to the Blessed Mother. For example, he could tell you how many rosaries it would take to walk from his house to the railroad yard where he used to work as an engineer. He had beautiful rose gardens and a grape arbor in his backyard.

Often, he would take my brother and me out for ice cream cones. I know that this did not sit well with my father, who was frustrated by my being overweight. Anyway, one day I came home from school—only to be informed that my grandfather had died suddenly that morning. I remember going to the funeral home and walking right up and reaching out and touching the hand of my grandfather's body. It was as if lightning had stuck! I never felt a feeling like that before. It left an indelible impression on my psyche. I also remember when it came time to close the casket. I was toward the back of the room. They wanted to take my grandmother out to the limousine. She resisted leaving my grandfather's body and she cried out in anguish—unlike any sound I had ever heard. Once again, it was as if lightning had struck; it left an indelible impression on my psyche. I knew right then and there, that something was very different about dying and death. There was more pain here than anywhere else.

Now, I would ask you to write all about your first experience of death. Try writing as much as you can possibly remember. It is important to reconnect with all of those memories now.

4

BEING
COMFORTED

Ever since I was a little boy, I wanted to be of help. As a child growing up in a Roman Catholic environment, I saw the priest as the designated helper. From a very early age, I knew that I wanted to be a priest. When I was in the eighth grade, I asked my father if I could go away to the seminary in order to study for the priesthood. He said "No!" He felt that if I had a vocation, I would retain it through high school and I could then enter at the college level. My father was right, and after high school I entered the seminary. To this day I am truly grateful to my dad for not allowing me to leave home at such an early age. As I reflect on it now, I think that I very much wanted to get away from home. I ended up having a great time in high school and making lots of friends. It made for a much more normal upbringing.

I went through college at St. Joseph's in Rensselaer, Indiana. I studied theology at Catholic Theological Union in Chicago (at that time a very liberal school of theology). I got ordained a deacon, which is equivalent to the internship for priesthood. I was stationed at St. Joseph's Catholic Church in Wapakoneta, Ohio. Thus I went from this liberal seminary in Chicago to this rather conservative, rural town in Ohio. I was quite a shock for those good people, and vice versa. Once again, the plaster fell from the ceiling as I entered this family system. The young people idolized me, while the older folks had a more difficult time understanding where I was coming from.

As a deacon, I was called upon to officiate at funerals, baptisms, and weddings. One young couple asked me to celebrate their wedding. Several months later, the young husband was shot and killed. I had to go to the funeral home; I knew there was nothing I could say that would take this young widow's pain away. Words would only get in the way! I went into the funeral home and stood next to her in front of the casket. I put my arm around her—just standing there silently. After a while, I held her somewhat more tightly and then turned and left—never uttering a word. Months later, she told me that that had been the most significant encounter throughout her ordeal.

Now, I would like to ask you to write all about an instance when another provided you with comfort in your time of need—either by what he/she did or what he/she said. Try writing as much as you can possibly remember. It is important to reconnect with all of those memories now.

5

TRAGIC
DEATH

Toward the end of my internship in Wapakoneta, I was asked to help out with the annual family retreat at the Maria Stein Retreat Center. They recruited me to work with the adolescents. Again, the kids just loved me, and the nuns were quite impressed. The Director asked me if I had ever considered going into retreat work after I got ordained. I told her "No"; however, the more I thought about it, the more it appealed to me. I had already had a taste of parish life. It had been rough for me. Retreat work sounded great. I went to my Provincial (my boss) and told him that when I got ordained I was going to work at the Maria Stein Retreat Center. He was flabbergasted. He was accustomed to telling us where to go and what to do. No other young priest had ever told him what he intended to do. I think he must have known that I was determined to have my own way. He just said, "Whatever you want to do, Father."

Now, I knew that I had a good thing going. I went back to the nuns and convinced them to let me sign a nine-month contract. I wanted to take the summer off and travel through Europe. They were so happy to have a priest who could relate to kids, they were willing to give me anything I asked for. I loved working at Maria Stein. In addition to working with the kids, I would often speak to groups of adults. One day a woman called me. She was from a nearby town and had heard me speak. She told me that her husband was dying in the Coronary Care Unit at a nearby hospital. She said that he did not get along with their parish priest and was not reconciled with the Catholic Church. She asked me if I would come and give him the "last rites." I told her that I would be glad to come and meet her husband.

I went to the hospital and introduced myself to her husband, "My name is Jack Miller. I am a priest from the Retreat Center; your wife asked me to come see you."

He said, "Thanks for coming, Father, but I really do not want to see a priest."

I replied, "I can understand that." Just as I was responding, the nurse in charge (who had been listening in on our conversation) came up to him and said in an agitated voice, "If you won't receive the last rites for yourself—then do it for me!"

Well, this man got so upset that he started vomiting. His monitors went wild. They came to me and said, "You will have to leave, Father." I went out to the waiting room, while they calmed him down and cleaned him up. I visited him three different times after that. He died very much at peace with God—even though he was not reconciled with the Catholic Church.

If you look at this situation symbolically, you find a psychologically healthy man who refused to swallow organized religion. It is important to make the distinction between God and religion. They are not one and the same! It is also important not to try to convert someone who is dying. They need our friendship—not necessarily our particular religious beliefs. I learned a great deal from this incident.

Not long after that I took $1,000 and headed for Europe for the summer. What began as a pleasure trip quickly developed into a pilgrimage. I grew increasingly lonely as I moved from country to country. By the time I got to Florence, Italy, I was so lonely that I was hurting physically. I prayed one evening that someone would come along to be with me and ease the pain of my loneliness. No one came that night. The next morning I was waiting in line at the train station to buy my ticket. I would always do this a day ahead of time, in order to assure passage on the train the following day. There was a young Italian fellow behind me in line. I did not speak to him because I was tired of frustrated conversations that did not go anywhere. As we got closer to the ticket booth, he began to sing in English. He sang, "Hey, Jude." I turned around and asked him if he spoke English. He said, "Yeah, I'm from New Jersey." We spent the entire day together. Toward the end of the day we were sitting on the cathedral steps, and I asked him where he had been born. It turned out that he had been born into the very same orphanage in Lackawanna, New York, as I had been born into! This was such a powerful answer to the prayer of the evening before that I could not act as if nothing had happened. As I continued on my journey, I began reflecting on how I had been demanding my way from the word "Go." Whenever I would get my way, I seemed to end up rather miserable. I reasoned that there must be another way.

I returned to the United States with one thin dime. I went to my Provincial and told him that I was willing to go wherever he wanted to send me. Once again, he was flabbergasted. He told me he would get back in touch with me.

Soon after that a young fellow was speeding on one of the country roads near Maria Stein, Ohio. This road was a favorite hangout of the local teenagers—especially after ballgames. The kids would park alongside this road and have tailgate parties—standing around the cars, sitting on the cars, and so on. That evening this young man ran a stop sign. He could not see what was on the other side of the hill beyond the stop sign. Suddenly, he found himself plowing through this group of kids—killing twelve in all. These kids were all from the town of Minster, Ohio. Most of them were related to one another. This was the worst calamity ever to befall that community.

There was no funeral home large enough to hold these bodies. They had to remove the pews from the sides of the Minster church and display the caskets there. The pastor had his hands full! He knew that I had worked with the kids from his church and that they idolized me. He called and asked me to help out. I told him I would come and have a Mass just for the teenagers the night before the funeral. No adult was allowed to be present. I went there that night and gave them permission to scream it out, shout it out, cry it out. And they did! The liturgy lasted approximately two-and-one-half hours. The next morning I had no energy left to attend the funeral. I only read about it in the paper the following day. The journalist remarked that "the teenagers were remarkably dry-eyed." I learned a lot about facilitating the grieving process that night.

Now, I would like to ask you to write all about some instance of tragic death that has touched your life in some way. Try writing as much as you possibly remember. It is important to reconnect with all of those memories now.

6

FUNERAL

On Ash Wednesday of that year, my Provincial asked me to think about serving as a parish priest in Cleveland, Ohio. On Good Friday, he came for my answer. I told him, "Yes."

Our Lady of Good Counsel (O.L.G.C.) was a large, multi-ethnic, inner-city parish. There were twelve Masses each weekend. The church building held eight hundred, and it filled to capacity for each Mass. I had gone from working with small groups in this idyllic rural environment to working with the masses in this sacramental factory. Almost immediately, I was asked to bury people whom I had never even met. At once, I set down a rule that I would not have any funeral without first meeting with the family. I felt it was very important to personalize the celebration of an individual's life. Whenever there is a death, the family is overwhelmed with details to attend to. By requiring that they meet with me, I interrupted their hustle and bustle, thus enabling them to get in touch with their feelings as they shared their loved one's story. Once again, I found myself helping to facilitate the grieving process. I had many funerals in Cleveland. I will share just one to give you a feel for what I am talking about.

It was one morning in late November, and this older woman had died. That afternoon the family came to see me. They told me she had been a ceramic artist, and that she had made nativity sets for each one of her grandchildren. I asked if I might see an example of her artistry. Later that afternoon, a young boy arrived with a box containing the crib set his grandmother had made for him. As we took out the figurines, I was moved by their beauty. I set them on my desk as a way to help prepare for the funeral two days later. As I studied the statues, I realized that she had not painted them with a brush. Her fingerprints were to be found in the paint on each of them. In preparation for the funeral, I took boxes and constructed a mountain scene by covering them with sheets. I arranged the statues at various heights on the mountain and placed lit candles in front of each one of them. The flicker of the flames against the figurines made them come alive with motion and light. During the celebration I talked about how this woman had not only left her imprint on the statues, but on every one there. The family was so moved that they gave me one of her madonnas as a gift. I, in turn, gave this to my parents for their Christmas gift. This is just one example of how I personalized the funeral celebrations.

Now, I would like you to write all about some funeral that really sticks out in your mind—a ceremony that spoke to you, either negatively or positively. Try writing as much as you can possibly remember. It is important to reconnect with all of those memories now.

7

PSYCHIC
PHENOMENA

I stayed at O.L.G.C. for a year and a half. My liberal training and unorthodox ways set me apart from the older priests. I just did not "fit in." I had tried surrendering to the will of my religious superior. It did not seem to work for me; therefore, I went out and found my own job as a hospital chaplain at Mount Carmel Mercy Hospital in Detroit, Michigan. There at the hospital, I was continuously being called upon to work with the dying and their family members.

Remember, the hospital system is geared to save lives. Death is seen as a defeat for the staff and the doctors in particular. In many ways, the dying are abandoned. Most hospital staff would rather invest energy in those who can "get better." Many mistakes are buried, and the families have no energy left to fight the system for a "better way to die."

I worked at Mount Carmel for a year and a half. I was often frustrated with death and dying in the hospital setting, but I did not know any other way.

I found priesthood to be too confining for me. I also found myself to be in growing ideological disagreement with the Roman Catholic Church—especially in regard to how women are treated. I made my decision to withdraw my services in protest. I set December 1, 1979, as my departure date.

Right after I let it be known that I would be leaving, I was approached by a hospice that was opening in Southfield, Michigan. They asked me to help pave the way for them by doing some public relations work promoting hospice. To this day, I do not know why they chose me. I did not even know what a hospice was. I told them I would do their work for them, if they would educate me. They sent me to the Hospice Institute in Connecticut. There I found answers to questions I had not even fully formulated. It was as if one door in my life was closing as another door was opening. I returned to

Detroit excited about hospice and helped to pave the way for the one opening in Southfield.

I knew that to leave the priesthood and deal with winter at the same time would be too much for me. A few years earlier, I had visited Mission Beach in San Diego. I phoned a friend of mine who lived near there and asked her to walk along Mission Beach and to call me with the telephone numbers of rental cottages along the beach. She phoned me with the numbers, and I set about calling around. Now, most of the cottages cost $800 to $900. I had $1,000 to my name. One place (a swinging single highrise) cost $350. I did not want to stay there. I was looking for a quiet place by the ocean where I could find some space for healing. Time was drawing near for me to leave; I could not bring myself to make arrangements at the highrise. It was a Friday in mid-November, and I was on call at the hospital that night. I decided that I would hold off until Monday and then call the highrise—even though I did not want to.

At 4:00 A.M., I was called over to the emergency room. A 93-year-old man had died and his 60-year-old son was there. The staff wanted me to spend some time with him. I went over and stayed with him for over an hour. He was handling things quite well; I said, "I think I will be heading home now, if you do not mind?" He asked me not to leave. He said that his sisters were on their way and he would like for me to be there when they arrived. I stayed and we began to talk about many different things. At one point I must have commented on the fact that this man was so very tan, and it was the middle of November in Detroit—long before tanning parlors were the rage. He said, "Oh, I have just come in from San Diego."

"Really? Why, I am looking for a quiet place to stay along the ocean out there. I am in need of some healing myself." Before I knew it, he made a phone call and arranged for me to stay at this retreat house north of San Diego overlooking the ocean. Within the walls of this place no spoken word was uttered. The meals were all vegetarian, and I stayed there for twenty-five days for free! If I had needed confirmation that I was embarking on the right path—this would have done it!

I took an entire year to go up the west coast. One of the things I did was to visit different hospices along the way. I returned to Chicago with the intention of developing a hospice training center in the midwest. A good friend of mine suggested that I further my education to best prepare for the task I had set myself to. I began by studying social work at Loyola University. My first class was Social Work with the Aging. Our assignment was to get to know an older person.

Elizabeth lived in my building, and she was ninety-three. I asked her if she would be willing to meet with me on a regular basis. She was most receptive to the idea. We met every Thursday morning for a banana pancake breakfast. As Elizabeth got to know me, she realized she could tell me things she had never shared with anyone else before. She had been a concert pianist and an artist. It turned out Elizabeth was also psychic.

She told me the story of her mother's passing. Elizabeth had been caring for her mother (who was dying) for quite some time. Toward the end, Elizabeth was exhausted. One evening she put her mother to bed in the adjacent room, and Elizabeth went to bed. Late that night she was awakened to a stream of light (coming from her mother's room) pouring through the wall and taking the shape of a giant egg at the foot of Elizabeth's bed. As she watched, more and more "etheric energy" filled the egg-shaped form. Two dark spots appeared within the egg; as she watched, they became more clearly defined as her mother's eyes. Elizabeth believes she was able to watch this for approximately forty-five minutes. Because of her exhaustion, she fell back to sleep. The next morning she got up to discover that her mother had "passed" during the night.

In all of my investigations of death and dying, I had never come across anyone who had witnessed this process. I asked Elizabeth if she would be willing to share this with the students in my school. She agreed.

It was not until several years later that I finally established The Center for Education on Death and Dying, Inc. As a student goes through The Center's ten-month process, he/she befriends someone who is dying. One of our students in the first year's class had been a Catholic priest. He left the priesthood, married, and had a family. He was befriending a former school teacher. He established a strong bond of friendship with this elderly woman. At times, he would even take his children along on his visits to her. At one point, he had to go to St. Louis for a convention. In his hotel room in the middle of the night, he was awakened to a light (but there was no lightbulb lit in the room). He was keenly aware of his dying school teacher friend. He noted the time. When he returned to Chicago, he was informed of his friend's passing. She died at the same time he encountered the light that night. I tell this story to give you permission to open up to such happenings. Our society does not encourage an awareness of psychic phenomena. Permission needs to be given in order for people to open up to these dimensions and see the light.

Now, I would like for you to write all about psychic phenomena that you have noted surrounding a death: for example, a clock stopping, an awareness of the dead person's presence, a dream around the time of death, whatever. It is important to reconnect with all of those memories now.

8

TRIBUTE MAKING

I have shared these stories from my own life as a way of getting you in touch with your own history of loss and deep-seated feelings. I know that it has not been particularly easy to dredge up all of these memories; however, getting in touch with your feelings does facilitate healing. Now, it is time to go one step further and create a tribute to your lost loved one. The creation of this tribute will help to heal your wounds and enable you to move on with your life. Let me explain the creation of a tribute by telling one last story from my own life.

It took five years to establish The Center in Chicago. Close to the time we were getting ready to open our doors, the *Chicago Tribune* ran a feature article on our school. Overnight, we had ninety-eight applicants for our first class. The *Tribune* received so many calls about our program, that without telling us, they ran the article on their wire service all over the country.

One morning I was at home, and the phone rang. This woman was calling me from Louisville, Kentucky. She told me that she had just read about me in the paper. She went on to say that her godson was hospitalized in Chicago with lymphoma. When she mentioned his name, I realized that I had known a fellow by that same name years ago in the seminary. She said that she thought one of our student's might benefit from visiting him, and vice versa. As she continued to talk, she mentioned that her godson had been a seminarian at one point in time. I told her I would visit him.

The man I met in the hospital was a mere shadow of his former self. We reminisced, and he informed me that he really had AIDS. Only his immediate family knew that he was gay. He was open to one of our students befriending him.

He lived alone, and when I brought the student to his home I saw that he was too weak to continue caring for himself much longer. I realized that housing was going to be an issue for him and others like him. I called some people together to establish a not-for-profit organization to provide housing for people with AIDS. We called it Chicago House—the midwest's first such residency program.

One of the individuals who came forward to help develop Chicago House was named Fred Woods. I liked him from the start. Fred was a wealthy publisher who also had been orphaned as a child and knew poverty all too well back then. He swore that he would never be poor again and worked very hard to build his empire. Fred was a compassionate man and went all out to see that Chicago House provided the very best for people with AIDS. He allowed us to use his business address as our mailing address and never failed to share his talents, resources, time, and influence championing this worthy cause.

Image was always very important to Fred. When I met him, he drove a '75 chocolate-brown Mercedes—a gorgeous classic car. He lived on the thirty-sixth floor of the Nieman Marcus Building—overlooking both the city and Lake Michigan. His condominium was decorated in shades of gray, and mirrored walls reflected the lake and the city from every possible angle.

As we worked closely together establishing Chicago House, our friendship deepened. Fred became my mentor—the older brother I never had. Several years into our relationship, he had a heart attack and had to have a quadruple bypass. I moved in with Fred for three weeks after he came home from the hospital. He was too weak to be left alone after his houseman went home at the end of the day. This time together bonded us for life.

Meanwhile, my father's health was deteriorating. He had had a massive stroke, which left him paralyzed on his left side. Mom had cared for him at home for a year and a half, and then she had a seizure, which was brought on by stress.

Dad had to be placed in a nearby nursing home; Mom could no longer care for him at home. All of this weighed on me as I was saving the dying of the world in Chicago! Finally, I just had to go home—there was no way around it.

Fred really did not want me to go; however, like my father, he too knew my stubborn side. I had to do what I had to do! I left for Ohio in the fall of that year. In early spring, I was notified that Fred died of a sudden heart attack one morning as he was preparing to leave for work. This was very difficult for me, as you can well imagine. After Fred's funeral I returned to our farm in Ohio. At that time, I was in the process of painting all of the buildings on the property. I decided to create my tribute to Fred by painting the buildings in shades of gray.

Our garage stands away from our house. There is a door on the side of the garage, which faces our house. It is not a garage door for cars but for people to walk through. I painted this door chocolate brown. I removed the window from the door and replaced it with a mirror that reflects the landscape and the sky. I had a plaque made; I placed it beneath the mirror. It reads, "The Fred Woods' Memorial Door." At the base of the door, I planted a rosebush. A while after that, a mutual friend of ours died. I planted a lilac bush in his honor by our house. It is reflected in the mirror on the Fred Woods' Memorial Door.

Image was never as important to me as it was to Fred. He always used to get on my case about being properly dressed for the theater or whatever. Now, as I walk out to the garage to go out for the evening, I'll stop by the door, look at my outfit in the mirror, and ask Fred if it meets with his approval.

This tribute has played an enormous part in my own healing process, and creating a tribute to your lost loved one can help to facilitate your healing as well. There are two specific instructions for you to follow:

>1. You must capture the essence of your lost loved one with your tribute.

>2. You must lose yourself in the making of the tribute.

For the greatest healing to occur, you must abide by these guidelines as best you can. I have witnessed many people heal their unresolved grief through the process of tribute-making. I know that it can work for you too.

Capturing the Essence

Capturing the essence of a lost loved one is no easy task. It requires lots of time and thought. This soul-searching puts you back in touch with this person's very being. You need to reconnect with this person's negative and positive aspects. You must focus on both this person's strengths and weaknesses. It is quite helpful to discuss your lost loved one with mutual friends and relatives. These discussions always help to expand your point of view.

There are as many ways to create a tribute as there are lives to celebrate. Some people choose to make a collage, or paint a picture, or carve a statue, and so on. I do not want to program your creative expression in any way by my suggestions or lack thereof.

Know that when you see your tribute, you will be reminded of your lost loved one. There is a real sense of communion in the presence of a tribute. I have seen the most wonderful tributes and heard the most remarkable stories about them, but I have told enough stories. Now, it is your turn to tell a story with your tribute. Let your tribute tell the story of the one you lost and still love.

Losing Yourself

Losing yourself in the making of the tribute is really the best part of this whole exercise. Once you have decided what you are going to make in order to capture your loved one's essence, you must then gather the materials. Having done that, you are ready to begin. Do take some measure to avoid being distracted. By that I mean that you should unplug the phone, etc., etc. It is really important to lose yourself in the making of this tribute. The best way to make sure that that will happen is to set yourself up so as not to be disturbed. I always tell people, "If you begin at 1:00 P.M. and finish up at 2:00 A.M., and you lost track of the time, then you did it!"

It is important to keep your tribute in a place of honor, where you can interact with it often. Several people have created panels for the AIDS quilt and sent them in—never seeing their panel (tribute) again. This only facilitates the healing process to a degree. These same people have had to create another tribute and place it where they can see it often; only then did they resolve their grief.

Afterword

It has been my privilege to accompany you on this journey. I would like to conclude by sharing with you the prayers that I have come to pray over the years. I find these prayers to be very meaningful and am glad to share them with you:

> Heal me, where I am in the deepest need of
>   healing.
> Grant that I might serve You with my life.
> Give me all that I need in order to do Your
>   will.
> Help me to become an effective instrument of
>   Your healing power.

These prayers basically sum it all up for me today. I am no longer demanding my own way, nor do I take direction from some outside authority. I listen to my inner guide by paying attention to my dreams and I strive to be true to what my inner guide calls me to. My stance today is a faith stance—a surrender to the unknown. I thank you for choosing me to accompany you on this healing pathway. Here's wishing you well, my friend.

Jack Miller, PhD

Other Books from Resource Publications, Inc.

GRIEF MINISTRY
Helping Others Mourn

Donna Reilly Williams & JoAnn Sturzl

Paper, $14.95, 232 pages, 5½" x 8½", ISBN 0-89390-233-0

An indispensable guide for anyone helping another through any type of loss, this book fills a frequently expressed need for an up-to-date resource that combines spiritual and psychological insights about griefwork. It covers general aspects of grieving, empathy, communication, listening, and prayer.

GRIEF MINISTRY FACILITATOR'S GUIDE

JoAnn Sturzl & Donna Reilly Williams

Paper, $19.95, 144 perforated pages, 8½" x 11", ISBN 0-89390-228-4

This *Facilitator's Guide* shows you how to set up a program to train grief ministers, using *Grief Ministry: Helping Others Mourn* as a textbook. The guide includes group listening and roleplaying exercises, scenarios for discussion, a resource listing, and photocopiable handouts.

MORGAN'S BABY SISTER
A Read-Aloud Book for Families Who
Have Experienced the Death of a Newborn

Patricia Polin Johnson & Donna Reilly Williams

Paper, $10.95, 72 pages, 7" x 10", ISBN 0-89390-257-8

Morgan's Baby Sister will assist parents and other adult caregivers in the difficult and often painful task of helping children understand their feelings about tragedies they experience. The read-aloud approach helps family members begin their recovery together.

Order these books from your local bookseller or directly from the publisher:

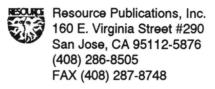 Resource Publications, Inc.
160 E. Virginia Street #290
San Jose, CA 95112-5876
(408) 286-8505
FAX (408) 287-8748

To your subtotal, add the following sales tax: 7¼% (California residents) or 8¼% (Santa Clara County residents). To that amount, add the following postage: $2 for orders up to $20; 10% of order for orders over $20 but less than $150; $15 for orders of $150 or more. Send check or money order to the address above.